Truth Be Told

Also by Linda Susan Jackson

What Yellow Sounds Like

Truth Be Told

Linda Susan Jackson

Four Way Books
Tribeca

for my granddaughter, Alanna Mei

Library of Congress Cataloging-in-Publication Data

Names: Jackson, Linda Susan, author.
Title: Truth be told : poems / by Linda Susan Jackson.
Description: New York : Four Way Books, 2024.
Identifiers: LCCN 2023031739 (print) | LCCN 2023031740 (ebook) | ISBN
9781954245969 (trade paperback) | ISBN 9781954245976 (ebook)
Subjects: LCGFT: Poetry.
Classification: LCC PS3610.A3532 T78 2024 (print) | LCC PS3610.A3532
(ebook) | DDC 811/.6--dc23/eng/20230721
LC record available at https://lccn.loc.gov/2023031739
LC ebook record available at https://lccn.loc.gov/2023031740

This book is manufactured in the United States of America and printed on
acid-free paper.

Four Way Books is a not-for-profit literary press. We are grateful for the assistance
we receive from individual donors, public arts agencies, and private foundations
including the NEA, and the New York State Council on the Arts, a state agency.

We are a proud member of the Community of Literary Magazines and Presses.

Contents

Prologue

IV

Epilogue

"But to find out the truth
about how dreams die, one should
never take the word of the dreamer."

—Toni Morrison

"A woman has a window in her face:
that is the truth. I look like my mother:
that is the truth. I want to tell you I am not
like her: that is the truth."

—Sara Borjas

Prologue

From Here to There

is a minefield fraught
With a dangerous freedom—

Step here: smell of menace
Step there: wearing hoods or heels

Here: year-old crimes & lotto tickets
There: *slow singing* & *flower bringing*

Here: sound of color's history
There: one woman becomes four

Here: words of a dreamer
There: calculus of nightmares

Step here: a familiar man's pup tent
Step there: baby formula on easy bake ovens

Here: rein in anything ready made
There: monopoly of meanings

Here: rag-wicked IED
There: t-shaped IUD

Here: hamlet to dismal swamp
There: cities of absence & erasure

Step here: a culture of data & optics
Step there: shadows with their own draw

Here: the past arranges its own past
There: oiled bodies spoon monotone

Here: tapping canes on the pavement
There: tragedy plus time is a drive-by

Here: the mother I longed for
There: the mother I had

Step here: light the fire
Step there: fire the cannon.

I

She was pure, Black, Noble,
Black, Blacker and Blacker Still."

—Kara Walker

Pecola's Juggernaut

Ugly is pretty
generic (there's enough to go around),
a name flung from the mirror I duck,
but I hear what it says: *Your living*
is complete defiance.

All of this was foretold in my history, shaped
by storefront living in my latchkey world.

My ugly is alive like a plague bred
on maternal distance & rage, on a father
itching to run & drowning in drink.

To be the ordinary ugly daughter
of a less than ordinary woman
is an accident that could have
crushed any girl & probably has.

Ugly is not my enemy; it's my private
deity, demanding worship from a song
that wets the wasteland my dry,
shocked voice has become, a song
that soars me off the ground
into the bluest sky
in my eye.

Chores

Cholly didn't shower me with gold or
swoop me up in a horse-drawn chariot.
I dreamt those things & add them when
I retell my story. He didn't shape-shift
into a bull, an eagle, or even a swan.
He was a buck with antlers that filled
the room. I was his prey. Blinded
by sunlight that streamed through
the kitchen curtains as he pounced
on me. Then. It was over. I was left
with the slurping sounds he made
in my ear & the feel of his body that
pinned me to the linoleum, smelling
like ammonia. It was Saturday, after all.

Ruint

Right now I can't see myself on the other side of this. They don't see me at all. My brother, Sammy, ran off. My father, Cholly, drowned in his whisky, and my mother, Mrs. Breedlove, I call her Polly now. Mostly, she's at church praying for all us heathens to her god who has forsaken me or she's with that white family she works for, them & their cherry wood furniture, their porcelain kitchen, their white dishes & the blueberry pies she makes for them. She blames me being ugly for everything, but if I'm so ugly, why'd he touch me? It's ok because when I'm fifteen, I'll be old enough to see my way clear to change my name to one that fits me. Pecola is a made-up name like Epitha or Rotissa, or Jamesetta. They shoulda left it at Peola or named me after a flower, like Peony or Pctunia. But guess what? I found a new name in the Big Black Book of Names— with it, I'll be beautiful, you'll see, not ruint like they say.

Like We Know

Claudia and Frieda tell me
it's their fault our marigolds
didn't grow. Claudia said
she knew "no green was
gonna spring from our seeds"
like she goddess of the garden.

.

Last season, the earth
was too hard to hold
seeds, just like my 12 year
old body was hard put
to hold my father's seed.

.

Soaphead Church, the so-called
interpreter of dreams, disappeared
from all he saw. & that mangy
dog, Bob, (who knew I was
supposed to kill him) read
my mind & ran off with it.

.

My mother, Mrs. Breedlove,
hates the sight of me since
I've "gone to seed" which
is how she explains
why I wander around
flapping my arms
screeching & screaming
at no one in particular
at everyone
at anyone.

.

Truth be told, like we know
something about seeds, jack-
leg preachers, marigolds,
still births, about whores
with place names, about
the snare of white, about
the cost of blue.

Pecola Questions Us

And if you answer

    who or what will I be,

        Cholly & Polly's slaughter or

            Trueblood's unnamed daughter

    me in free fall

        the womb or tomb

    words of worth

        shadow or sight

    monument or memory

        sentiment or sentinel

    myth or magic

        some rye or a sweet lie?

    Are you my true eye?

Camera-Ready

"I am and shall continue to be the monster in your closet."

—*Kara Walker*

From the great
disrupter
of fairy tales,
the story of me
is inevitable.

Bored
with your damsels
who live their lives
under a knife
or a needle,

Racked
by thoughts
of a future
that consumes
so much
of a black
girl's life,

Already adultified.

.

What language
can remember me
from before
the funk
of your fears
lodged
to discomfit?

      .

Who do I wait for,
      three Gorgons or
            The Three Whores,
      three Furies or
            The Three Degrees,
      three Peace women or
            The Mary Jane Girls?

      .

Who knew
eyes held
my doom,
slingshot
from every gaze?

Camera ready?
I am Pecola
Breedlove,
Still.

Dear Miss Chloé Miss Toni Morrison,

I don't mean no disrespect Miss Chloé, but you don't know me. *We're gonna have to explain to her how we feel about being the root of her story.*

It's me who gets teased, beat up, or completely ignored. *They see us or don't see us, despise us on sight or with just the thought of us.*

I'm that girl: black. *Blue-black is the term they use.* Skinny with ashy legs and ugly. *All the things people loathe.*

Miss Chloé, you say you love me, so why didn't you give me another mother? *She could have given us Pilate or Sethe, mothers who wanted to save their daughters. They showed real courage.*

Why didn't you let Mrs. MacTeer keep me? *She smiled at us and sang songs on Saturdays.* She only fussed when I drank all the milk. *Mrs. Breedlove beat us to make our black less black.*

What do I have **but** my skin? *We're black dust, collecting on what's most hated: girl, poor, black, and ugly.*

Miss Chloé, you gave me a lot to deal with. *Twists and turns down the crookedest streets in the world, searching for marigolds and plucking at any kind of blue.*

You had me pray for a miracle every night. *She only let us see ourselves in other people's eyes, their anger, their disgust, their fear—their nothing!*

High-yellow dream girls still get everything. *How they loved Maureen Peal who enchanted them with her sloe-green eyes and copper-colored braids cascading down her back.*

Why couldn't they love **me**? *Maybe if we were one thing—black or ugly, but both? Where's our Shug Avery?*

I still don't know why you wrote that book about me. *You made our life a curse of wounds that didn't kill but didn't heal either.*

Nothing changed for me. *We roam these streets day and night. Folks stare and then look away. We growl our hunger at them.*

Maybe one day, Miss Chloé, you won't ever need to write about a girl like me. *Humph. The world ain't ready for a story about a black girl with a voice and a future.*

Yours truly,
Pecola Breedlove

Scene One, Take Two

Scene:

Mrs. Breedlove is from an aristocracy
of dreamers. Unable to afford a TV,
she'd lose herself for twenty-five cents
in a darkened theater, relish the high
wall it built around her at matinee time.
In there, she's Deborah Kerr, racing
to meet Cary Grant at the top of
the Empire State building, or Audrey
Hepburn ready to sacrifice her throne
after a few nights with Gregory Peck,
or Miiko Taka for whom Marlon Brando
risks his Air Force career. This realm
of dreams, a *terra incognita*, takes her
so close to an imitation of Lana Turner
who also lived life like a character in film.

Take:

She'd kidnap the screen stories & imagine a life
for herself, fence with Hollywood fancy like a Doña
Quixote, romp in lives way out of reach for a young
colored woman saddled with children & day's work.
When the double feature ended, she remained seated
until the theater was empty. The matrons worked
around her, sweeping between rows in the balcony.
Her cue was the whirr from the projector, preparing
for the next feature while a ray of white light flickered
down from the projection booth. Getting up, she
stumbled until she found her mark. Even Jack Cardiff's
rhapsodic use of color in *The Red Shoes* couldn't paint
over what she faced when she left the theater,
adjusting to the reality of the hazy, setting sun.

Sun-born

O, she of sun-born blackness
whose story is the one we want
to pass like the night. What
does this explain except our
hunger for a dozen Maureen

Peals although when we're done,
we throw them on the heap
of over-handled things, using
what's left of their skin to pass
on the story. Our hunger, still

afire as we go on with our usual
business. It's Pecola's story
we want to get past, a past
that's the mirror of our
present & to be rescued from

watching her slow retreat into
madness. She's just 12 years
old, standing by herself, without
a weapon to wage war, without
a rage to sustain her, stepping

out of an unwritten history into
the underbelly of a girlhood,
under the crush of colorism
where knowing her father's
name is not enough.

View-Master

1. Click

This old man, he played three…

Without worry, she bounces
on his trusted lap. He whispers.

His breath in her ear is
like candy on her tongue.

A grope here. A paw there.
Undercover, gutter delight.

He played knick-knack on my knee.

2. Click

Here we go looby light…

She gets carried away, rocked
by ballad rhythms in her ear.

Sheet pulled down, he blank-
ets her. Touches everywhere.

Dream drifting, floating out there.
One kiss. One finger. One pluck.

All on a Saturday night.

3. Click

You put your whole self out…

His breath, his hands.
Hot solid in liquid.

She sobs & drops from the sky. Her
voice stalls while she's in free fall.

That's what it's all about.

4. Click

Miss Mary Mack, Mack, Mack…

She nearly strangles on her nightgown. Panties
tie up her ankles. She can't even run in place.

His voice, begging, demanding
Don't tell. No longer a lullaby.

All dressed in black, black, black.

5. Click

Mary, Mary quite contrary...

Day after, her flesh is bereft, yet
she breathes. If only she could fly.

Zeely's on the shelf. So is Ramona.
All that's past. No one's to know.

How does your garden grow?

Dear Pecola (part 1),

For some time, I've wanted to write to you especially since I had written **about** you and because you came to me with your questions about love and beauty and hate and about those confounded blue eyes you yearned for so desperately. Initially, I was repelled by your desire for blue eyes and by the fact that you said you wanted the bluest eyes of all.

Dear Pecola (part 2),

It took me a long time to block out all the noise from the voices of those who crave what is white, blue-eyed, and blond-haired. Their desire is so strong because they're convinced fair skin equals beauty equals success equals love. This longing for blue eyes didn't begin with you, baby. It lies dormant and returns with a vengeance every decade or so as though new.

Dear Pecola (part 3),

Truth be told, I wrote the book for both of us. I wanted to understand more about the strength of your extravagant wish plus I had my own questions. For instance, how had you come to believe blue eyes would make all the difference in your world? I wanted your life to matter, so I did the best I could against the tide to break down silences that implicate so many.

Dear Pecola (part 4),

More than anything else, I wanted to expose who and what left you without protection and broke you so completely. Plus, your wish was so earnest, so innocent, I couldn't resist.

Baby girl, my dear, sweet Pecola, please know that I love you **best** and **most** because you were **first.**

Always,
Miss Chloé

II

"Wholeness is no trifling matter."

—Toni Cade Bambara

More Than Drylongso

—*after my great-grandmother*

New brooms sweep clean, but old brooms know the corners

In and out of paradise, it starts with a disturbance in the nourishing dark of sound that becomes a wail, then rises into words, into song, giving rhythm and story to living and loving. At least, that's the plan, though it's so easy to go off in the wrong direction, to be in such a hurry, you pour coffee in your purse and can't grasp the enormity of a rhetorical break. But you've been here before, following a crooked straw lined to where it angles and cleans the corners of others, and you do what you know.

Stick with the evil you know

Everything she learned was picked up walking from tobacco country to the cobblestones of New York. Carrying a barlow in her purse, she later marries off her one son to a woman who carries a pistol in hers. They are outlaw women, wearing silk dresses and pearl-buttoned gloves, pretty women who dab lilac water behind their ears and a knee. They are dangerous and free. They know the sound of action is their voice, and volume is its value, yet they whisper "Evil be pretty sometimes, don't it?"

Don't trade a monkey for a black dog

   She considers this since the monkey asks questions for his blasted survey: why this, why that, how would you, on a scale of 1 to 5, rate the black dog in the cast iron frying pan or is he in the fire? Is the monkey a bird in the hand or is the black dog in the bush? Does the monkey drink from a glass half full or does the black dog lap at his half empty bowl?

Buzzard don't circle in the air for nothin'

The rest of them picked what was easy and flew off, but he's still circling. He's been at it a while, so she glimpsed the swoop and swirl of his fancy eights; caught the streaks of light from his diamond-encrusted talons; heard the swish and whistle of his wings, him crowing out that Nat King Cole favorite, "Darling, Je vous aime beaucoup," which left him just enough wind for his final dive, to get a closer look and see if she's the wild game they talked about or just another piece of side-meat.

She ain't washed in the same water

Though she knows how to boil peach leaves and Sampson snakeroot to lower the fire that burns so brilliant it blinds, the crime is already on the floor. Her hair clumped in hall corners, she prowls their old haunts in crowds of strangers looking for the start of an angry flood or her leading man. Basted in the seams of a new dress, underneath the rick rack, there's another story sorting the coloreds from the whites, lingerie from linens, from what has to pre-soak and what needs mild agitation, so she can keep her shape and still draw out all the stain.

Still water won't make a string of pearls

She lives in a world of grit and spit, no bells or whistles herald all she does to wrap her private circle in layers of luster. Her beauty emerges over time, so he waits, trying his best to coax her from the shiny coat she's out growing. In a little too deep and under pressure, she demurs, stringing him along as she's done with so many others. He whispers. The ripple from his plea closes her up, still and tight.

Ain't but a poor mouse got but one hole

    With an eye trained on him for a few years, give or take a day, she watches him stockpile women who speak a pentimento of nuance, warning him they'll make him leave his name in the bushes. But pride burns him down like roux stuck to cast iron. The sea is calm, tufts of white float in a sunlit sky, streaked with ribbons of beryl, aquamarine. He is rum-high. Hints of mint on his tongue unfurl her violet wings with a whisper and drip ruin on the road. He and his songs, all renegade. First a ballad, then a piece of blues. What do they prove?

Give 'em a book and they never learn

She was a great mystery to her parents, though she lived
with her mother who was, at times, indifferent to her. They
first ask, "What part of your body that daughter of yours
come from?" Then claim, "She look like him, walk like
she know everything." But she was really only interested
in a piece of the story, something beautiful or tragic, that
makes her tense or tear up, for music with range, like
Sarah or Nina, not all peppermint and perfume, for what
is found between the covers.

Same meat, different gravy

   She remembers when her Daddy was buried with his Sears Silvertone not more than a stone's throw from where the spreading oak she loved as a child was cut down, leaving a stump scar in the earth and her heart, changing her natural phrasing into a jungle of gestures. Then there was his music: a voice with many faces. Within his song, she made sense of the world, a motion of events seduced by too much silk or a new impulse. She came to know new meant same difference.

A hat and a shoe don't make a pair

From a tangle of legends, she emerged, barely thirty-five, she'd already buried three husbands. He came out of the blue with no rules, a slab of Bushmills in his pocket, his cuffed pants breaking just above the third eyelet of his spit-shined, ox-blood leather shoes. So their lives fold in on one another. They talk and laugh their way through clubs with fancy sounding names like *Paradis, Alcazar, Le Palais*, their insides dark. A thousand nights later, she'd given him almost everything and could only hear what was in front of her—him and his escape words: "Honey... Dahlin'...Baby Girl, I'll be right back." She should have read the signs earlier since he belonged nowhere in particular, since he always kept his fedora, its crown creased like a tear drop, perched on the right knee of his crossed leg.

Everything don't need to be told

Afraid to fly, she gestures through the wind with imaginary tree limbs. A white handkerchief, scalloped with lace, spills out the pocket of her housecoat with strings that hang like fringe. Her eyes, rimmed in teal blue, eyebrows still arched, thick and black. Her beauty, once said to be excessive, saved her from day's work but not from the day-to-day. Birthdays lost in song, in too many loves gone wrong. She clears her throat and the smoke from all the bars in her head. And her words "that motherfucker," sharp as orange moonlight shot through a swamp of tupelos.

III

"…he never asked if I would stay,
which is why when the choice appeared,
I reached for it."

—Rita Dove

"Suppose my punishment
was fields of lilies sharper than razors,
cutting up fields of lies…"

—Sally Wen Mao

Persephone Meets Pecola

Searching
for any sign
of spring,

I spot her
out the corner
of my eye.

She's a bag
of water.

I bend down,
hand her
my handkerchief

& ask why
she's sad.

Pounding
the ground,
she yells

the marigolds—
they didn't grow.

I sit with her
until her body
stops heaving.

Pulling her closer,
I whisper, "There
are flowers

more beautiful
than marigolds."

She states more than
asks *how you know?*

Enfleurage

"How to smell like a flower without being plucked."
—*Yona Harvey*

I try but can't avoid flowers. They throw
all their purity at me. Top notes lure me
into plummy pools that evaporate quickly,
leaving a smooth combination of fruit &
floral, yielding to a final full body of fragrance,
typical during the dry down period of aromatic
grass, wood & musk's lasting impressions.

It's near morning & like jasmine & tuberose,
I've been open all night. The dew dries, releasing
soft sweet scents scored as sin in my skin,
alive with volatile weather. This is not
a crime, yet. Just the vanity of drooping
flowers shouting spring. Somewhere between
daffodil & narcissus, this could be you, too.

Nowhere to Run

Weekly I go to the garden
          with my two best friends.
          We inhale its beauty,
revel at its symmetry.
I wander off with my music.

My friends swoon
          to silky falsettos
          or toned-down tenors.
I prefer a front man
who knows how to attack silence,

craving a church-trained
          tenor like Eddie Levert
          whose gruff-edged, gospel
tones fling me out
of my body or a preacher's

son like Dennis Edwards,
          unafraid to plunge
          into gritty excess.

I am so rapt by the
intensity of their pleas,

by the certainty of their
        promises of a love
        rare as a rose in winter
I don't hear
my friends call out.

When the ground splits
        open, I mistake
        the rumble for a backbeat.
Just like that he snatches
me up & out of the world

of rhythm & ballads.
        He doesn't pretend
        to sing, hum, or recite
a lyric. The only sounds
in the bloom-heavy air

are the high-pitched
        neighs of his black
        stallions, heads aimed
to burrow their way
back to his dark realm.

Center Stage

1.

When I return to her, she acts
like it'll forestall the grand
fall of autumn, the inevitable
wilt after Labor Day. She
doesn't see I'm not the dutiful
12-year-old daughter she lost.
I'm queen of my own realm
now, but she still calls me
by my pet name, "Sephie,
you'll never be grown."

2.

She parades me around, brags
how she demanded my release
(yes, you & I know it's only
for a few months out of the year—
so let's just humor her). "I don't
get Sephie back, they'll be no green
for your mortals," was her threat

for months on end. Many suffered
& starved that first year.

3.

When I went missing, I thought my
father would roll up in his Lancia
B50, the black coupe with its cognac-
colored interior & rescue me, not end
up bargaining with his brother (who
reminded my father how he helped
him defeat the Titans). Promises made.
Gifts exchanged. My uncle becomes my
consort. Rita Dove writes, "There are
no laws when laws are broken."

4.

The other thing is my father's
always distracted. He simply
loves beautiful women & my
mother puts up with his shit. She

throws tantrums, threatens to leave;
she even had children with her own
side-piece. Then complains my father
could break anything but his habits.
Yet she stays.

5.

Home was never a stable concept
for me, so it holds little memory.
I was mostly rootless which is why I
love the garden, why I love flowers.
Their blood is in the soil & like seeds,
I spend a lot of time underground.

6.

When I first opened my eyes, I thought
I had on a blindfold or had gone blind.
It was as black as the middle in a bucket
of tar. I was square in *the midnight hour*
when there's no one else around though there

was a faint smell of *Old Spice*, maybe even
a whiff of spikenard? Images flutter past,
streaks of blue light from his precious
metals. "What do I call you?"

7.

He'd heard stories of old men who lost
everything, some lost their heads, others
their lives, so he groomed me only for
himself. He downloaded all of my music
to soothe my delicate flesh that, for months,
grieved for my mother. His pageantry
made me dizzy & he blinded me with
bling. What's a girl, now a goddess, to do?

8.

Four months is the longest I can resist
the crushing pull of his gravity. I return
to my gilded queendom freshened
by frolic & fun, shore & sun. Still

can't figure out why he chose me.
I didn't launch one ship. No one ate
an apple because I said *try it*. I wasn't
carved out of a single slab of marble.
I was just 12, dancing between flowers.

Persephone's Theory

"You can't leave 'cause your heart is there
but sure you can't stay 'cause you been somewhere else."

—Sly & The Family Stone

Quiet as it's kept, my mother & father
are divinity, but they are also brother &
sister: wife & sister = the same woman^2.

    This makes my father my uncle
    & my mother my aunt: daughter
    & niece = the same girl^2.

At last count, I have twenty
some odd sisters & brothers—
both my parents are players!

    So my siblings are like cling
    peaches in heavy syrup: all
    halves = nothing whole^2.

My father's brother is also my mother's
brother; he kidnapped, raped, & married
me: niece & wife = the same captive^2.

    With him, my children = (cousins & nieces
    & nephews)^2 & to my parents (his siblings)
    they = (grandchildren & nieces & nephews)^2

so close yet so far
removed that the speed
of light wobbles around

        the mass of branches
        on my family tree
        & can't square

enough variables
to equal who or
what is relative.

Sephie's Clock of the Long Now

After I wind it every which way, each moment
  takes dominion everywhere, sprinkling its pleasure
    & doubt beyond the earthy complexity of black

Truffles, the elegant restraint of a dark-skinned
  Syrah, or the gaudiness of a Maybach parked
    on a street with an uncertain future. Is time

Random or a sequence of events? Is it an event
  or a wheel, the thing occurring or what has already
    happened from today to a millennia ago? I'm

Going back & forth at the same time, along
  all points on the line, updating myself as I go,
    so I'm open to remember or forget the mythic

Past, amassed & bent. If I hurry, time will slow
  down to a place where it stands watch, where
    every day is Saturday, but if this is a split screen

Or another scheme, there's not much for me to do
  but read obituaries looking for my father. At what age

Did I realize life leads to a place between dog &

      wolf, what miracle of me survives here in deep time?

When Persephone Has the Blues

This is how she prays—
alone, at dusk, whispering
mercy, then grows still.

Weathered yellow lights
stew down with her blues, burning
wisteria's scent.

With but a whisper
tears cut a hot path of lines—
her face in fragments.

A bird in the night
flies her song through the darkness—
tremolo in blues.

Whisper the answer—
was she ruined before now
or in the garden?

IV

If you're silent about your pain, they'll
kill you and say you enjoyed it."

—Zora Neale Hurston

Girls to Women

—for Sheila

An unlikely pair of high-toned girls
meeting when we did, you, thirteen

with your brash language, playing
hooky, and me, twelve, with a book

under my arm. You, already smoking
on the sly, your hair dyed blonde

like one of Dinah's wigs, and me,
shoulder-length twin braids, in class.

We, in training bras, our calves shaped
by double dutch and hand ball, longing

for Smokey to build us a castle with his
falsetto, for Ivan Dixon, black-dark

and handsome in *Nothing But a Man*.
Are we game for the men who dress

like high stakes, leaning against a liquor
store window, whispering *pig meat?*

Girls to Women Redux

We are now the age
our mothers were

when we thought
they were old

becoming them
despite ourselves

despite our need
for a man's touch

no paladins
or galahads.

.

Are we meeting
again as though

for the first time
this you, worrying

about crow's feet
& double chins

this me, worrying
about the blackness

of black & syntactical
trots, this us worrying

about the algebra
of our broken parts?

Lost & Found

After decades with no history
& my voice stuck from strain
That I sing at all is a mystery.

Lives piled like props in scenery
Thrown up to camouflage pain
Of decades with no history.

Chant now sequel to melody
Whose sound drums with the rain
That I sing at all is a mystery.

What's left is part eulogy
For bones sunk in tough terrain
After decades with no history.

Ululations score my mutiny
& summon an ancient refrain
That I sing with all its mystery.

Canticle for my destiny
With the blues—no need to explain.
After decades with no history,
That I sing at all is a mystery.

Threnody

—for Dinah Washington (1924-1963)

When she started out
she welcomed the road,

moved as she was to be
anybody but Ruth Lee Jones,

game as she was to let go
of Alabama and lives
hemmed in by hemp,

to live in a world teeming
with every song she sang.

On stage, stylized in satin,
she's a veneer of calm.

Her voice, clear as raw triumph,
muscles colors from her throat—

the best brights:
halters and halos,

the darkest darks:
she's drinking again,

her neck already
ringed in sweat.

Home was anywhere she was,
caught between gut-bucket
blues and *Blue Gardenia,*

though not even duets with Brook Benton,
hundreds of singles, seven, eight or was it

nine (?) husbands could blot out
shot-gun houses on cinder blocks,

mossbacks in back woods
or yard boys scared of trees.

May 12, 2009

Dear Miss Etta James,

With only the tap & growl
of a flamenco guitar, you open

with *A Lover Is Forever* & girl,
you hollow out the room.

Every booth, every table taken. Folks
stacked four & five deep at the bar.

You know it all because you've
done it all & we take what you give

over trombone, trumpet, & sax;
piano, organ & box; one son,

Donto, on drums, the other,
Sametto, on bass guitar.

You hit all the money notes.
Your rough edge wide & deep;

even with a love song, you're
face down in gravel, talking

shit on your way to the grit
in the final song. There,

a new blue—throaty &
true. But, you didn't listen

baby girl, when Billie said
Don't let this happen to you.

And you did. You did.

Sum of the Parts

If you have a minute, walk this hour with me,
      anywhere and remind me
            how deep laughter can reach.

You begin talking; at least, I see
      your mouth move, but I can't
            hear the parts you say.

.

I ask *What is your quarrel with the world?*

You say *Damn woman, you make a man wanna travel.*

.

We laugh, a nervous laugh, realizing there are too many
      moving parts, and we haven't been moved in years.

The roles we thought important, aren't.

        Ah, the time we spent being them.

    .

Crepe myrtles line our path,

      oaks form a canopy,

          roses overgrow the trellis

             that once trained them

upright, and you say something

      about life being part love

         and part theft.

Who burned the bridge between our falls?

Nailing Things Down

may also kill them,
      but she had no great plans
            to live happily ever after.

Today is all she could manage,
      that & the breathless sounds of Pres,
            tamping down the day's anarchy.

Twenty years earlier, her voice left her,
      so she quit smoking. When it returned
            it was vibrating like a dusty contralto.

Today she smells facts:
      the air thick with tomorrow's rain,
            a slow leak in the basement.

The five shots of Jameson on his breath.

      His undershirt brushed with
            someone else's perfume, a scent
                  she'd worn in high school—*Shalimar.*

Twenty years ago, on a dime,
      she'd have cut or shot him to clear

the air, but today is not that day.

Today she looks at her body
    with some hesitation. It's late
        in the morning & the gravy's
            gonna run thin tonight.

Will she miss the wanting, the having or the gone?

On the Lower Frequency

—for Jayne Cortez (1934–2012)

she pitches sound into
the unexplored slant
against the deep while
the bass player follows
his pluck a cue to leap into
the silence between breath
& syllable since the drum
is a woman certain as
yearning she vibrates
like dark stars of a cosmos
swirling up a circular set
her call shapes & creates
the grace notes we crave
with plenty skin all we
need to know is the time
she says we're in

What Good Is a Castle

—*after Joe Bataan*

In the mirror, I'm no longer there,
But the someone who is looks at me

As though surprised that I show up
Every morning. What else is there to do?

I've become my own curio, a daily novelty,
Trying to work magic with foundation,

Blush brush and lipstick which yields no
Promise, so when the image turns away,

It takes apart my voice. No matter.
No one ever listens when I speak.

Stunned by the ticking clock, I stare back
In the mirror. All the markers are gone.

I am what was both bounty and beauty,
Added value to the trinity for young skin:

Possession, performance, profit!
There's no running from it. Once

My beauty could choke the scarlet
Off a rose, almost predict the edge

Of the world, make music out of what happened
Although everything changes with the playing,

Worrying the line to dust. I'm in time's geography,
So what's left of its shifting melody, a breath, a note,

A glance, a new ache? Outside, everything
smells of week-old grease, even the clouds.

Why'd She Turn?

Because she smelled the morning's fresh bake

Because she'd lived a life without trouble

Because she heard a familiar voice yell her name

Because every yard, every street held a memory

Because she'd not been warned directly

Because she longed to see her daughters & grands

Because she lingered over the fence, over dinner

Because she didn't fear for her own safety

Because the bird must turn to take the egg from its back

Because she'd heard about the *futility of wandering*

Because a mother's need differs from what an angel wants

Because Lot always bragged about his God's grace

Because she had Eve's blood

Because who wouldn't?

Epilogue

"Only Earth—wild mother we
can never leave… knows no
story's ever finished."

—Rita Dove

Main Sequence

As a star ages, I'm hooked
on its deep music in a room

with Monk on repeat, one foot
in his galaxy & the other in dreams

of death & I marry, of fish & I give
birth, of weddings & I grieve. Then,

like pillars of creation, a barrage of
questions throws my instincts off

balance, making all my forfeitures visible,
task by task, reflex by reflex since now lays

age open to equal parts mask & a revelation:
beauty works until it doesn't, falling away

as surplus to aches, to the letting go,
driven by forces of gravity then flight,

leaving a hunk of ash in its wake, an
imprint of wrinkles & perspiration,

stretch marks of wear & tear
my black body once there.

Acknowledgments

I would like to acknowledge the following journals and audio archive where some of these poems have appeared: *Academy of American Poets Poem-a-Day Series, Harvard Review, Mission on Tenth Inter-arts Journal, Obsidian: Literature in the African Diaspora,* and *Ploughshares.*

With humility and all my heart, I wish to thank my maternal ancestors who send the light:

mother   Lillie May Monroe (b. 1931)
grandmother   Jessie Royster (b.1915)
great grand   Lillie May Gordon (b.1894)
great grand   Minnie Wheathersbee (b.1880)
2nd great grand   Mary Portis (b.1845)
3rd great grand   Jacky Morgan (b.1820)
4th great grand   Disa Morgan (b.1785)

I give special thanks and much gratitude to EA, LS Asekoff, Kwame Dawes, Tyehimba Jess, A. Van Jordan, John Murillo, Nicole Sealey, and Tracy K. Smith for their advice and encouragement as these poems were taking shape.

I shall always be grateful to Toi Derricotte, Cornelius Eady, founders of Cave Canem, and all the workshop leaders, fellows, and staff at Cave Canem…and Dante Micheaux.

I draw inspiration from everything: art, music (especially music), literature, history, myths, family stories, nature, and from everyone who was and who is in my life—family and friends. All Love.

Much thanks to Martha Rhodes, Ryan Murphy, and the Four Way team for their care and attention bringing this book to life.

Abundant thanks to JoAnne McFarland for creating the baby girl, "Armed and Considered Dangerous," who graces the cover of this book.

I would be remiss if I did not express my gratitude and deepest appreciation to Toni Morrison whose rich words live within me and to Rita Dove whose stunning poems in "Mother Love" helped me focus.

Finally and always, I am deeply grateful to my husband, Rodney, who has, for nearly fifty years, given my life so much love and helped me truly understand what it means for someone to have your back, and to our son, Rod, and his wife, Margaret. This trio continues to enliven and strengthen me with their unequivocal love and support. Yo soy, porque nosotros somos (I am because we are)!

Linda Susan Jackson is the author of *What Yellow Sounds Like* (Tia Chucha Press), a finalist for the National Poetry Series and the Paterson Prize and two chapbooks, *Vitelline Blues* and *A History of Beauty*, both published by Black-eyed Susan Publishing. She has received fellowships from the Cave Canem Foundation, the New York Foundation for the Arts, Calabash International Literary Festival, Soul Mountain Writers Retreat and The Frost Place. Her work has appeared in *Brilliant Corners: A Journal of Jazz and Literature*, Center for Book Arts Broadside Publications, *Crab Orchard Review*, *Harvard Review, Heliotrope*, *Los Angeles Review, Mission at Tenth Inter-arts Journal, Obsidian: Literature of the African Diaspora, Ploughshares*, and *Rivendell*, among others, and has been featured on The Academy of American Poets *Poem-a-Day* Series, and *From the Fishouse*. She's a retired associate professor of English from Medgar Evers College/CUNY.

WE ARE ALSO GRATEFUL TO THOSE INDIVIDUALS WHO PARTICIPATED IN
OUR BUILD A BOOK PROGRAM. THEY ARE:

Anonymous (14), Robert Abrams, Michael Ansara, Kathy Aponick,
Michael Anna de Armas, Jean Ball, Sally Ball, Clayre Benzadón,
Adrian Blevins, Laurel Blossom, Adam Bohannon, Betsy Bonner,
Patricia Bottomley, Lee Briccetti, Joel Brouwer, Susan Buttenwieser,
Anthony Cappo, Paul and Brandy Carlson, Dan Clarke, Mark Conway,
Elinor Cramer, Kwame Dawes, John Del Peschio,
Brian Komei Dempster, Patrick Donnelly, Lynn Emanuel, Blas Falconer,
Jennifer Franklin, John Gallaher, Reginald Gibbons,
Rebecca Kaiser Gibson, Dorothy Tapper Goldman, Julia Guez,
Naomi Guttman and Jonathan Mead, Forrest Hamer, Luke Hankins,
Yona Harvey, KT Herr, Karen Hildebrand, Carlie Hoffman,
Glenna Horton, Thomas and Autumn Howard, Catherine Hoyser,
Elizabeth Jackson, Linda Susan Jackson, Jessica Jacobs and
Nickole Brown, Lee Jenkins, Elizabeth Kanell, Nancy Kassell,
Maeve Kinkead, Victoria Korth, Brett Lauer and Gretchen Scott,
Howard Levy, Owen Lewis and Susan Ennis, Margaree Little,
Sara London and Dean Albarelli, Tariq Luthun, Myra Malkin,
Louise Mathias, Victoria McCoy, Lupe Mendez, Michael and Nancy
Murphy, Kimberly Nunes, Susan Okie and Walter Weiss,
Cathy McArthur Palermo, Veronica Patterson, Jill Pearlman,
Marcia and Chris Pelletiere, Sam Perkins, Susan Peters and
Morgan Driscoll, Maya Pindyck, Megan Pinto, Kevin Prufer,
Martha Rhodes and Jean Brunel, Paula Rhodes, Louise Riemer,
Peter and Jill Schireson, Rob Schlegel, Yoana Setzer,
Soraya Shalforoosh, Mary Slechta, Diane Souvaine, Barbara Spark,
Catherine Stearns, Jacob Strautmann, Yerra Sugarman, Arthur Sze and
Carol Moldaw, Marjorie and Lew Tesser, Dorothy Thomas,
Rosalynde Vas Dias, Rushi Vyas, Martha Webster and Robert Fuentes,
Abby Wender and Rohan Weerasinghe, Rachel Weintraub and
Allston James, and Monica Youn.